main courses
& side dishes

WILLIAMS-SONOMA

main courses & side dishes

WELDON OWEN

contents

introduction

For many of us, on an average evening the main course is the only course we prepare.
It may be a favorite stir-fry or pasta dish, an easily cooked piece of chicken or fish,
or a one-pot meal of soup or stew. But when we have time for ourselves and our
families, or when entertaining, the side dishes we choose come into equal importance
as complements to the main dish in the overall dining experience. When main meets
side artfully, there is perfect harmony on the plate and dinner is served.

—chuck williams

vegetarian

In light of modern dietary wisdom, most people know that a break from meat as a main course is a good idea. As many meat and nonmeat eaters alike have long known, and as reflected in many of the world's great cuisines, delicious things can happen when vegetables, eggs, cheese, and grains take on the dominant role in a main dish. From the fresh flavors of Herb Nettle Ravioli to light and delicate Individual Stilton Soufflés and hearty Endive Chowder, these inspired vegetarian dishes demonstrate the enormous variety of meatless—but never boring—mains.

Individual Stilton Soufflés

Stilton cheese adds a rich bite to the traditional Gruyère flavor for these picturesque individual soufflés. Handle the egg whites gently to ensure a good puff.

1½ teaspoons unsalted butter, plus 2 tablespoons, softened

2 tablespoons dried bread crumbs

2 tablespoons finely ground walnuts

1 tablespoon finely grated Parmesan cheese

½ cup (2½ oz/75 g) all-purpose (plain) flour

1 cup (8 fl oz/250 ml) milk

4 egg yolks, lightly beaten

1 cup (4 oz/125 g) shredded Gruyère cheese

salt

cayenne pepper

7 egg whites, at room temperature

1 tablespoon fresh lemon juice

¾ cup (3½ oz/105 g) crumbled Stilton cheese

SERVES 5

1 Place a baking sheet in the oven and preheat to 375°F (190°C).

2 Generously butter inside of five ¾-cup (6–fl oz/180-ml) soufflé dishes with 1½ teaspoons butter.

3 Mix bread crumbs, walnuts, and Parmesan together and divide between buttered dishes. Coat dishes completely with crumb mixture. Tip out any excess and refrigerate until needed.

4 In a bowl, work flour and 2 tablespoons butter together with a fork or your fingers to form a smooth mass.

5 Bring milk to a boil in a saucepan over medium heat. Whisk in flour-butter mixture and return to a boil, stirring until thick. Once thickened, remove from heat and stir vigorously until smooth. Transfer to a large bowl and let cool.

6 When soufflé base is cooled, stir in egg yolks, Gruyère, and pinches of salt and cayenne. Set aside.

7 In a bowl, using an electric mixer, whisk egg whites, lemon juice, and a pinch of salt at high speed until soft peaks form. Gently fold in Stilton.

8 Whisk one-fourth of egg whites mixture into soufflé base to lighten mixture. Carefully fold in remaining whites.

9 Fill prepared soufflé dishes to top with mixture and smooth with a knife. Run your thumb along inner rims of dishes to push mixture slightly away from sides.

10 Place on hot baking sheet and bake for 15 minutes.

11 Raise oven temperature to 400°F (200°C) and bake until puffed and golden brown, 7–10 minutes longer. Serve immediately.

Kabocha Squash, Broccoli, and Yellow Beans

2½ lb (1.25 kg) kabocha squash

1 lb (500 g) yellow beans, trimmed

1 lb (500 g) broccoli, cut into florets, stems trimmed and sliced

1 tablespoon peanut oil

2 cloves garlic, minced

1 teaspoon minced red serrano chile

2 teaspoons peeled and finely chopped fresh ginger

salt

2 teaspoons soy sauce

2 tablespoons pine nuts

SERVES 4

As this nutritious vegetarian stir-fry demonstrates, winter squash doesn't have to be relegated to long-baked or heavy dishes. Also try other combinations such as brussels sprouts, spinach, and carrots. If you're short on time, use the same boiling water to blanch the vegetables individually, removing them with a slotted spoon.

1 Using a large, sturdy knife, halve the squash lengthwise. Scoop out seeds and fibers. Slice halves into wedges. Rest a wedge skin side down on a cutting board and gently carve flesh away from peel. Repeat with remaining wedges, then cut peeled wedges into slices ¼ inch (6 mm) thick. Set aside.

2 In separate saucepans of lightly salted boiling water, blanch squash, beans, and broccoli until tender-crisp. Drain and set aside.

3 Heat oil in a wok or large skillet over high heat and toss and stir garlic, chile, and ginger for 30 seconds.

4 Add squash, beans, and broccoli. Toss and stir for 2 minutes. Add salt to taste, soy sauce, and pine nuts. Sauté for 3 minutes longer. Serve immediately.

Herb Nettle Ravioli

Nettles have long been used in Europe as an alternative to spinach or kale; substitute spinach here, if you prefer. Garnish these tender homemade ravioli with big, pretty shavings of Parmigiano-Reggiano, if desired.

12 oz (375 g) nettle leaves

2 eggs

½ teaspoon sea salt, plus more to taste

2 cups (10 oz/315 g) all-purpose (plain) flour, plus more if needed

1½ cups (12 oz/375 g) ricotta cheese

¼ cup (1 oz/30 g) freshly grated Parmigiano-Reggiano cheese

¼ cup (1 oz/30 g) freshly grated pecorino romano cheese

½ cup (¾ oz/20 g) *each* finely chopped fresh flat-leaf (Italian) parsley and fresh chives

freshly ground white pepper

rice flour, for sprinkling

5 tablespoons (2½ oz/75 g) butter

1 tablespoon extra-virgin olive oil

1 cup (8 fl oz/250 ml) vegetable stock or chicken stock

SERVES 4–5

1 Using tongs, plunge half of nettle leaves into a large pot of boiling, salted water. Drain as soon as wilted and dark, bright green. Press out excess moisture and finely chop. In a bowl, combine chopped greens, 1 egg, and ½ teaspoon sea salt.

2 On a work surface, mound 2 cups flour, make a well in center, and pour in greens mixture. Using your fingers, drag in flour from edges to combine. When all flour has been combined, begin to work it into a unified mass. Texture should be slightly dry. If it seems too dry, add a few drops water. If too sticky, work in a little more flour. Knead until dough is silky, about 15 minutes. Cover with a bowl or plastic wrap and let rest for 45 minutes.

3 While dough is resting, combine 3 cheeses with remaining egg in a bowl. Stir in parsley and chives. Season to taste with sea salt and white pepper. Set aside.

4 Divide dough into 4 equal pieces and roll out each on a pasta machine, ending with finest or next-to-last setting. Dough must be thin, but not too thin to hold filling; each sheet will be about 18 inches (45 cm) long. Trim edges and lay sheets on a work surface sprinkled with rice flour. Working with 1 sheet at a time, fold lightly lengthwise to make a center crease and open again. Drop teaspoonfuls of filling every 3 inches (7.5 cm) down center of 1 half. Fold other half of dough over mounds and press firmly around filling with your fingers to seal. Using a ravioli or pastry cutter, cut into squares. Put them on baking sheets sprinkled with rice flour. Repeat with rest of dough for 20 ravioli total. Bring a large pot of salted water to a boil.

5 While water is heating, in a wide skillet, melt butter in oil. Add remaining nettle leaves and pour in stock. Simmer until greens are tender. Drain, season to taste with salt, and divide among shallow individual bowls.

6 Lower heat for pasta water to a slow boil. Add ravioli and cook until tender, about 2 minutes. Transfer to bowls with a slotted spoon and serve immediately.

Blue Cheese, Pear, and Walnut Quiche

all-purpose (plain) flour, for dusting

Pâte Brisée (page 124)

2 ripe pears, preferably Bartlett
(Williams'), peeled (optional),
halved, cored, stemmed, and cut
lengthwise into slices ¼ inch
(6 mm) thick

1 cup (4 oz/125 g) crumbled
blue cheese

½ cup (2 oz/60 g) walnut halves,
roughly chopped

½ cup (4 fl oz/125 ml) milk

½ cup (4 oz/125 g) crème fraîche

1 egg, lightly beaten

salt and freshly ground
black pepper

SERVES 4–6

The classic combination of cheese, pears, and nuts goes into this quiche made in a tart pan. To unmold, set the tart pan atop a canister and let the sides fall away.

1 On a lightly floured surface, roll out pâte brisée about ¼ inch (6 mm) thick and line a 10-inch (25-cm) round fluted tart pan with a removable bottom. Trim edge. Using a fork, prick base. Cover with plastic wrap and refrigerate for at least 1 hour or overnight.

2 Preheat oven to 375°F (190°C).

3 Line chilled tart shell with parchment (baking) paper or aluminum foil and fill with pie weights or dried beans. Bake until sides are set, about 10 minutes. Remove weights and parchment or foil. Continue baking until bottom is set, 5–10 minutes longer. Remove from oven and let cool.

4 Raise oven temperature to 425°F (220°C). Arrange pears, blue cheese, and half of walnuts in baked tart shell. In a bowl, beat together milk, crème fraîche, egg, salt, and pepper until combined. Pour into tart shell. Sprinkle remaining walnuts on top.

5 Bake tart until filling is just set and golden brown on surface, 30–40 minutes. Let cool on a wire rack for 30 minutes before unmolding and serving.

Risi e Bisi

½ lb (250 g) green (spring) onions, including a few pale green tops, cut into 2-inch (5-cm) pieces

2 cups (3 oz/90 g) packed spinach leaves

2 tablespoons packed fresh flat-leaf (Italian) parsley leaves

¼ cup (2 fl oz/60 ml) olive oil

1 cup (7 oz/220 g) Vialone Nano rice

5–6 cups (40–48 fl oz/1.25–1.5 l) vegetable stock or chicken stock, heated

1½ cups (7½ oz/235 g) shelled English peas (about 1½ lb/750 g in the shell) or frozen peas

kosher salt and freshly ground black pepper

fresh Parmesan cheese shavings, for garnish

SERVES 4

For this Venetian spring dish, use enough stock so that the rice-and-pea mixture remains soupy. Vialone Nano is a tiny, almost transparent short-grain Italian rice; you can also use Arborio.

1 In a food processor, finely chop (but do not purée) green onions, spinach, and parsley.

2 In a large saucepan over high heat, heat olive oil. Add rice and sauté for 2 minutes. Reduce heat to medium. Add stock, a ladleful at a time, stirring frequently, until about half of stock has been added and absorbed, about 15 minutes.

3 Stir in peas and chopped green onion mixture. Continue adding stock and cook until peas are tender, about 5 minutes. Consistency should be soupy; add more stock if needed.

4 Season to taste with salt and pepper. Garnish with Parmesan cheese shavings and serve immediately.

French Onion Soup

1 tablespoon unsalted butter

1 tablespoon olive oil,
plus more for brushing

5 large onions (about 2 lb/1 kg
total weight), thinly sliced

¾ cup (6 fl oz/180 ml) *each* dry
white vermouth and dry white wine

6 cups (48 fl oz/1.5 l) vegetable
stock or 3 cups (24 fl oz/750 ml)
each chicken stock and beef stock

1 teaspoon finely chopped
fresh thyme

1 bay leaf

salt and freshly ground
black pepper

¼ cup (2 fl oz/60 ml) dry sherry

twelve ½-inch (12-mm) slices
day-old sourdough baguette

6 tablespoons (1½ oz/45 g) grated
Parmesan cheese

1½ cups (6 oz/185 g) shredded
Gruyère cheese

finely chopped fresh chives,
for garnish

SERVES 6

The onions are key in this bistro classic. Have patience and allow them time to become soft and caramelized over low heat. Serve with a green salad and a glass of wine.

1 In a large skillet, melt butter with olive oil over low heat. Add onions. Cook, stirring often, until caramelized, about 45 minutes. Transfer to a soup pot.

2 Add vermouth and wine to skillet, stirring to scrape up browned bits from bottom of pan. Cook to reduce liquid by half. Add to onions. Stir stock into pot. Add thyme, bay leaf, and salt and pepper to taste. Simmer gently for 15 minutes to incorporate flavors. Add sherry and cook about 5 minutes longer. Discard bay leaf.

3 Meanwhile, preheat oven to 350°F (180°C). Line a baking sheet with aluminum foil and brush lightly with olive oil.

Place bread slices on lined baking sheet, brush with olive oil, and season to taste with salt and pepper. Top each slice with 1½ teaspoons Parmesan. Bake until crisp, about 15 minutes.

4 Preheat broiler (grill). Divide hot soup among 6 ovenproof crocks. Float 2 croutons on each crock. Sprinkle each with ¼ cup (1 oz/30 g) Gruyère.

5 Broil (grill) 2 inches (5 cm) from heat source until cheese starts to melt and brown, 2–3 minutes.

6 Garnish with chives and serve.

Endive Chowder

4 heads Belgian endive
(chicory/witloof)

1 large yellow-fleshed potato

2 turnips (about ½ lb/250 g)

2 leeks, white part only

2 tablespoons unsalted butter,
plus more for toast

2 shallots, diced

2 celery stalks with leaves, diced

2 large carrots, peeled and diced

2 teaspoons minced fresh
thyme leaves

1 bay leaf

5 cups (40 fl oz/1.25 l)
vegetable stock or chicken stock

salt and freshly ground
white pepper

½ cup (4 fl oz/125 ml) heavy
(double) cream

2 tablespoons finely chopped fresh
flat-leaf (Italian) parsley

1 tablespoon slivered chives

1 teaspoon chopped fresh tarragon

3 slices country-style bread

SERVES 4

This mixed-vegetable soup is similar to the French *potage bonne femme*, but the endive's mild bitterness gives its flavor a slight edge. The soup can be dressed up or down to fit the occasion: purée most of the vegetables for a smooth, sophisticated first course, or leave them whole for a chunky soup ideal for a casual supper.

1 Set aside 8 outer leaves of endive, then quarter and coarsely chop remainder. Peel potato and dice into small cubes. Peel turnips and cut into chunks. Chop leeks and rinse well.

2 In a wide soup pot, melt 2 tablespoons butter over medium-high heat. Add chopped endives, potato, turnips, leeks, shallots, celery, carrots, thyme, and bay leaf. Cook over medium-high heat, stirring frequently, until vegetables are fragrant and there is a little glaze on bottom of pot, about 7 minutes.

3 Add stock and 1½ teaspoons salt. Bring to a boil, then reduce heat and simmer, covered, until potato is soft to point of falling apart, about 25 minutes. Discard bay leaf. Press a few potato cubes against side of pot to break them up, or transfer about one-third of vegetables to a blender and pureé, then return to pot. Add cream. Season to taste with white pepper. Taste and add salt, if desired.

4 Finely sliver reserved endive leaves. Stir half of parsley, chives, and tarragon into soup. Toast bread, butter it, and cut into small cubes to form croutons. Ladle soup into bowls. Top with croutons, remaining herbs, and slivered endive.

fish & shellfish

The inspirations for the dishes in this chapter are the fishermen who bring their fresh catch to ports around the globe and immaculate, whole fish and steaks or fillets on display at the best seafood markets. The recipe for Pistachio-Crusted Fish Fillets combines a rich, nutty crust with the light, evocative flavor of halibut fresh from temperate ocean waters. The cold waters of the Northern Atlantic are the source for the fish in Cod, Leek, and Stilton Pie, a quintessential British dish, and tiny anchovies, so beloved in the Mediterranean, bring salty tang to Tomato and Anchovy Tart.

Pistachio-Crusted Fish Fillets

A rich and crunchy crust is the perfect complement to moist fish fillets. Serve with oven-roasted vegetables and a squeeze of fresh lemon juice.

4 firm white fish fillets such as
halibut, cod, or sea bass,
5–6 oz (155–185 g) each

salt and freshly ground
black pepper

¾ cup (3 oz/90 g) shelled whole
pistachio nuts, finely chopped

½ cup (1 oz/30 g) fresh bread
crumbs, preferably made
from French or Italian bread,
including crust

1 tablespoon chopped fresh lemon
thyme or English thyme

1 tablespoon unsalted butter

2 tablespoons olive oil

SERVES 4

1 Preheat oven to 400°F (200°C).

2 Season fillets with salt and pepper.

3 In a shallow dish, combine nuts, bread crumbs, and thyme. Toss gently to mix.

4 Working with 1 fillet at a time, dredge both sides of fillets in nut mixture, pressing gently to form a thick crust.

5 In a large, ovenproof sauté pan, melt butter in olive oil over medium-high heat until hot. Arrange fillets in pan without crowding and cook, turning once, until just golden, 3–5 minutes total. Transfer to oven and bake until fillets are opaque throughout, 5–7 minutes longer, depending upon thickness. Using a metal spatula, carefully invert each fillet onto a warmed dinner plate and serve at once.

Cod, Leek, and Stilton Pie

PASTRY

3½ cups (17½ oz/545 g)
all-purpose (plain) flour

¼ teaspoon salt

1 cup (8 oz/250 g) cold unsalted
butter, cut into small pieces

2 eggs

1 lb (500 g) cod or scrod fillet

salt and freshly ground
black pepper

2 cups (16 fl oz/500 ml) milk,
or as needed, plus 1 tablespoon

6 tablespoons (3 oz/90 g)
unsalted butter

3 leeks, white and pale green parts
only, sliced into rings

freshly grated nutmeg

3 tablespoons all-purpose
(plain) flour

½ cup (2 oz/60 g) crumbled
Stilton cheese

¼ cup (2 fl oz/60 ml) heavy
(double) cream

1 egg

MAKES SIX INDIVIDUAL 5-INCH (13-CM) PIES

The mild flavors of leek and cod come into focus when combined with sharp Stilton cheese. Be creative with cutting decorations from dough scraps, if you're inclined.

1 FOR PASTRY: In a food processor, combine flour and salt. Pulse in butter until mixture resembles bread crumbs. Pulse in eggs. With motor running, add enough very cold water to make a soft dough, 5–6 tablespoons. Form into 2 disks, 1 slightly larger than the other, wrap each in plastic wrap, and refrigerate for at least 30 minutes or overnight.

2 Place fish in a large sauté pan and season with salt and pepper. Cover with 2 cups milk, or more if needed, and bring to a simmer over medium-high heat. Cook until fish is just opaque and flakes easily, about 10 minutes. Drain, reserving cooking liquid. Flake fish, discarding any bones, and set aside. Strain milk and set aside.

3 Heat 2 tablespoons butter in a skillet over medium heat. Add leeks with a sprinkling of nutmeg and cook until softened, about 5 minutes.

4 In a saucepan over medium heat, melt remaining butter. Add flour and stir to a smooth paste. Slowly stir in 1¾ cups (14 fl oz/430 ml) reserved milk and continue to cook, stirring often, until thickened and smooth, 8–10 minutes.

5 Add Stilton and stir until blended. Stir in cream. Taste and adjust seasoning. Gently stir in flaked fish and leeks. Remove from heat and set aside.

6 Preheat oven to 350°F (180°C). Have ready six 5-inch (13-cm) pie pans or ovenproof ceramic bowls.

7 On a lightly floured surface, roll out larger disk of dough about ¼ inch (6 mm) thick. Using a pie pan as a template, cut 6 rounds of dough slightly larger than inverted pan to form bottom crusts. Line pans with rounds and refrigerate for at least 20 minutes. Roll out second disk and trace inverted pie pan to make 6 tops. Place tops on a baking sheet lined with parchment (baking) paper and refrigerate until ready to use.

8 Divide filling among lined pie pans. Apply top crusts and seal edges. Lightly beat together egg with 1 tablespoon milk and brush tops. Cut small vents in pastry and decorate with glazed pieces of scrap dough as you like. Bake until golden, about 45 minutes.

Tomato and Anchovy Tart

Inspired by the ingredients of the Provençal staple *pissaladière,* this savory tart makes a delicious lunch or dinner entrée.

all-purpose (plain) flour, for dusting

Crunch Dough (page 124)

1 tablespoon olive oil

1 small onion, finely chopped

1 or 2 cloves garlic, finely chopped

8 plum (Roma) tomatoes (about 1½ lb/750 g total weight), peeled (page 125), seeded, and coarsely chopped

salt and freshly ground black pepper

pinch of herbes de Provence

1 tablespoon tomato paste

3 cups (1 lb/500 g) mixed small tomatoes such as cherry, golden, and grape, thinly sliced

½ cup (2½ oz/75 g) pitted Kalamata olives, sliced

6 anchovies in olive oil, drained

1 tablespoon extra-virgin olive oil

fresh Parmesan cheese shavings, for garnish (optional)

SERVES 4–6

1 On a lightly floured surface, roll out the crunch dough about ¼ inch (6 mm) thick and line a 12-by-4-inch (30-by-10-cm) rectangular fluted tart pan with a removable bottom. Trim edges. Using a fork, prick base. Cover with plastic wrap and refrigerate for at least 1 hour or overnight.

2 In a large skillet, heat olive oil over medium heat. Add onion and cook until soft, about 5 minutes. Stir in garlic and cook for 1 minute. Add tomatoes, salt and pepper to taste, herbes de Provence, and tomato paste. Cook, stirring often, until mixture has thickened, 25–30 minutes. Remove from heat and let cool to room temperature.

3 Preheat oven to 375°F (190°C).

4 Line chilled tart shell with parchment (baking) paper or aluminum foil and fill with pie weights or dried beans. Bake until sides are set, about 10 minutes. Remove weights and parchment or foil. Continue baking until bottom is set, 5–10 minutes longer. Remove from oven and let cool.

5 Raise oven temperature to 425°F (220°C). Place baked tart shell on a baking sheet. Spread tomato mixture evenly over bottom of tart shell. Cover with tomato slices, olives, and anchovies. Drizzle with extra-virgin olive oil.

6 Bake until crust is golden and tomatoes have caramelized in places, about 30 minutes. Serve warm or cold, garnished with Parmesan shavings, if desired.

Sole, Pea, and Artichoke Gratin

Serve this hearty gratin with green beans or a simple green salad. Soaking in lemon water prevents the artichokes from browning.

1½ teaspoons unsalted butter, plus more for gratin dishes

½ lemon

10 oz (315 g) skinless sole fillets

1½ teaspoons extra-virgin olive oil

salt and freshly ground black pepper

2 slices bread, crusts removed

½ cup (2 oz/60 g) grated Parmesan cheese

6 baby artichokes, stems intact

½ cup (4 fl oz/125 ml) dry white wine

¾ cup (6 oz/185 g) crème fraîche

1½ cups (8 oz/250 g) canned or frozen baby peas

SERVES 2

1 Preheat oven to 400°F (200°C). Lightly butter 2 individual gratin dishes.

2 Finely grate zest of lemon half. Reserve lemon. Cut sole diagonally into ½-by-4-inch (12-mm-by-10-cm) strips and place in a shallow dish. Add olive oil, lemon zest, and salt and pepper to taste. Cover and marinate in refrigerator for at least 15 minutes or up to 1 hour.

3 Place bread slices on a baking sheet and bake until dry, about 10 minutes. Break into pieces. In a food processor, pulse to fine crumbs. Toss with Parmesan and set aside. Leave oven on.

4 In a large bowl filled with cold water, squeeze in juice from ½ lemon and add squeezed lemon half. Remove outer tough leaves of baby artichokes. Cut off top ½ inch (12 mm), trim stems, and cut into quarters. Submerge in lemon water until ready to use. (If using globe artichokes, cut tops off to reveal hearts, spoon out choke, and cut into eighths.)

5 Bring a saucepan of lightly salted water to a boil. Drain artichokes and add to boiling water. Return to a boil, reduce heat, and simmer for 5 minutes. Drain and place in a small bowl.

6 In a large skillet, melt 1½ teaspoons butter over medium heat. Add sole with its marinade and cook, stirring occasionally, for 2 minutes. Add artichokes and cook for 2 minutes longer. Divide sole and artichokes between prepared gratin dishes. Set aside.

7 Add wine to skillet, stirring to scrape up browned bits from bottom of pan. Stir in crème fraîche. Cook over high heat until sauce is slightly reduced, about 3 minutes. Reduce heat, add peas, and cook until sauce thickens, 2–3 minutes. Divide between gratins. Sprinkle tops with crumb mixture. Bake until golden brown, 10–12 minutes.

ood

MARKET

RESTAURANT

IF IT SWIMS WE HAVE IT

VE HAVE IT

Roast Cod and Vegetables

1 cod fillet, about 1½ lb (750 g)
and 1½ inches (4 cm) thick

¾ teaspoon caraway seeds

10 strips thinly sliced bacon

8 bay leaves

2 tablespoons extra-virgin olive oil

18 pearl onions, blanched
and peeled

1 lb (500 g) baby potatoes such
as Yukon gold, scrubbed

6 cloves garlic, unpeeled

2 heads baby fennel (about
8 oz/250 g total weight), trimmed

4 baby leeks, trimmed

1½ cups (3 oz/90 g)
cauliflower florets

½ teaspoon whole coriander seeds

salt and freshly ground
black pepper

6 oz (185 g) baby asparagus or
thin young asparagus, trimmed

SERVES 4

A bacon crust gives this slow-roasted cod a savory second dimension. Choose young, tender vegetables for the accompaniment that brings new meaning to "garden variety."

1 Preheat oven to 400°F (200°C).

2 Place cod on a large sheet of plastic wrap. Sprinkle caraway seeds over cod. Wrap bacon around cod so that it covers evenly without overlapping; if using fish that is unevenly thick, tuck thinnest part underneath, then cover with bacon. Secure with kitchen string. Slip bay leaves between bacon slices. Drizzle with 1 tablespoon olive oil, wrap plastic wrap tightly around fillet, and refrigerate until ready to cook.

3 In a large flameproof casserole, heat remaining 1 tablespoon olive oil over medium heat. Add pearl onions, potatoes, and garlic and sauté for 5 minutes. Add fennel, leeks, cauliflower, coriander seeds, and salt and pepper to taste and cook for 5 minutes longer, gently stirring occasionally with a wooden spoon.

4 Add asparagus and ½ cup (4 fl oz/ 125 ml) water to casserole and transfer to oven. Roast until liquid has reduced and vegetables are roasted and slightly browned, about 40 minutes. Remove skins from garlic and return to casserole. Set aside and keep warm.

5 Meanwhile, remove plastic wrap from cod. Transfer cod to a baking dish and roast until fish is opaque and cooked through, 30–35 minutes. When both fish and vegetables are done, remove from oven and preheat broiler (grill). Slip fish under broiler and broil (grill) fish until bacon is crisp, 1–2 minutes. Transfer to a platter and remove string. Slice and serve with vegetables.

Globe Zucchini
Stuffed with Crab

1 red or yellow bell pepper (capsicum)

12 globe zucchini (courgettes) or regular zucchini about 2 inches (5 cm) in diameter

2 tablespoons olive oil

1 red onion, finely chopped

2 tomatoes, peeled (page 125) seeded, and finely chopped

1 teaspoon red wine vinegar

1½ teaspoons finely chopped fresh flat-leaf (Italian) parsley

1½ teaspoons finely chopped fresh mint

1½ teaspoons finely chopped fresh chives

¼ lb (125 g) fresh lump crabmeat, picked over for shell fragments

½ cup (1 oz/30 g) coarse fresh bread crumbs

salt and freshly ground black pepper

SERVES 4–6

More and more produce sections stock globe zucchini, a round variety about the size of a softball that's perfect for stuffing. If you can't find them, substitute regular zucchini. This dish makes a light main course or a substantial side.

1 Preheat broiler (grill). Put bell pepper on a baking sheet and roast, turning several times, until skin is blackened and blistered all over, 15–20 minutes.

2 Transfer bell pepper to a paper bag. Close bag and let stand until cool, 10–15 minutes. Peel off blackened skin. Slice pepper in half lengthwise and remove stem, seeds, and ribs. Chop finely and set aside.

3 Preheat oven to 400°F (200°C).

4 Cut tops off globe zucchini and set aside. (For regular zucchini, slice one-third off lengthwise.) Scoop out flesh with a spoon, leaving walls ¼ inch (6 mm) thick. Finely chop flesh and set aside.

5 Have ready a bowl of ice water. In a saucepan of lightly salted boiling water, blanch zucchini shells for 2 minutes. Plunge into ice water, then drain and set aside.

6 In a large skillet, heat 1 tablespoon olive oil over medium heat. Add roasted pepper, onion, tomatoes, and reserved zucchini flesh and cook until softened, 4–5 minutes. Add vinegar and cook for 2–3 minutes longer. Remove from heat and let cool. Stir in herbs, crabmeat, and bread crumbs, and season with salt and pepper to taste.

7 Stuff zucchini shells with crabmeat mixture; do not overfill. Place in a baking dish and replace the tops. Add ½ cup (4 fl oz/125 ml) water to dish, drizzle zucchini with remaining 1 tablespoon olive oil, and bake until tender and stuffing is cooked through, about 30 minutes.

Salmon Pot au Feu

Salmon replaces beef in this French classic that is an elegant main course and side dish all in one. Fleur de sel is French sea salt.

4 baby carrots, trimmed and halved lengthwise

4 white baby turnips, trimmed and halved

4 small creamer or other starchy potatoes, peeled and halved

4 skinless salmon fillets (5 oz/155 g each)

salt and freshly ground black pepper

2 cups (16 fl oz/500 ml) chicken stock

4 green (spring) onions, cut into 1½-inch (4-cm) lengths

½ cup (1 oz/30 g) brussels sprout leaves

1 tablespoon unsalted butter

2 tablespoons minced chives

fleur de sel

extra-virgin olive oil, for drizzling

SERVES 4

1 Preheat oven to 350°F (180°C).

2 In a saucepan of lightly salted boiling water, blanch carrots until barely tender, about 2 minutes. Using a slotted spoon, transfer to a bowl and rinse with cold water. Repeat process with turnips, blanching for about 5 minutes. Return water to a boil, add potatoes, and cook until tender, 8–9 minutes. Drain and set aside.

3 Season salmon fillets with salt and pepper. Place salmon and stock in an ovenproof skillet and bring stock just to a boil over high heat. Cover and transfer skillet to oven. Bake until salmon is almost opaque throughout but still slightly pink inside, 8–10 minutes.

4 Leaving stock in skillet, carefully transfer fillets to a warmed platter. Simmer stock over medium-high heat for 5 minutes. Add carrots, turnips, potatoes, green onions, and brussels sprout leaves. Return to a simmer and cook for 1 minute.

5 Divide salmon and vegetables among warmed individual bowls. Whisk butter and chives into stock and pour over fish. Sprinkle with fleur de sel and drizzle with extra-virgin olive oil.

poultry

The versatility, ease of cooking, and appealing flavor of chicken have made it the perennial first choice for poultry dishes. But to take advantage of the many similarly pleasing options in the poultry category, this chapter includes recipes for Cornish hens, a hybrid miniature chicken, as well as guinea hen, squab, and goose. All these birds make great eating with their deeply flavored flesh and are just as easy to prepare. For that all-important dinner in late November, we offer the ultimate juicy Brined and Roasted Turkey, a preparation that deserves to be a Thanksgiving classic on any table.

Cornish Hens with Honey Glaze

Guajillo and mesquite honeys come from desert country and have mild, very distinctive flavors. Look for them online or in specialty-foods stores.

butter, for baking dish

2 Rock Cornish hens
(1 lb/500 g each)

sea salt

1 tablespoon olive oil

2 tablespoons guajillo or
mesquite honey

zest from 1 lime and juice
of 3 limes

1 teaspoon ground cumin

1½ teaspoons mild red chili powder
or sweet or hot paprika

freshly ground black pepper

SERVES 2

1 Place a rack in upper third of oven and preheat to 400°F (200°C). Lightly butter a baking dish just large enough to hold both hens.

2 Rinse hens and pat dry. Rub well inside and out with sea salt. Tie legs together with kitchen string and fold wings underneath body. Transfer birds to prepared baking dish.

3 In a bowl, combine olive oil, honey, lime zest and juice, cumin, and chili powder. Taste and adjust seasoning, if needed, with sea salt and pepper. Pour mixture over birds and baste to coat well.

4 Bake, basting about every 10 minutes, until an instant-read thermometer registers 160°F (71°C) when inserted into thickest part of leg, 45–50 minutes. Glaze should become thick and glossy. Serve hot, warm, or cold.

Stilton and Smoked Duck Salad

1 bunch baby beets,
stems trimmed to 1 inch (2.5 cm)

½ cup (4 fl oz/125 ml) walnut oil

4 teaspoons champagne vinegar

1 teaspoon Dijon mustard

½ teaspoon fresh lemon juice

salt and freshly ground
black pepper

1 bunch (8 oz/250 g) watercress

2 firm but ripe pears, cored and
cut into thin slices

3–4 oz (90–125 g) smoked duck
breast, thinly sliced

¼ lb (125 g) Stilton cheese,
thinly sliced

SERVES 4

Walnut oil—used for flavor, not for cooking—is somewhat expensive, but a little goes a long way in making a rich and interesting dressing. Serve the vinaigrette on the side, if you prefer. Smoked duck breast is available in specialty-meat stores and many well-stocked supermarkets.

1 Preheat oven to 375°F (190°C). Place unpeeled beets in a baking pan. Pour water into pan to a depth of 1 inch (2.5 cm). Cover pan with aluminum foil. Bake until beets are tender, about 40 minutes.

2 Remove beets from pan and let cool until easy to handle. Peel and quarter, then set aside.

3 Whisk together walnut oil, vinegar, mustard, lemon juice, and salt and pepper to taste in a small bowl.

4 Place watercress in a bowl or on a platter. Add beets, pears, smoked duck breast, and Stilton. Just before serving, pour vinaigrette over. Toss gently and serve immediately.

Coq au Vin

½ cup (4 oz/120 g) unsalted butter

1 lb (500 g) cipollini onions, blanched and peeled

1 lb (500 g) small white mushrooms, wiped clean and stemmed

2 tablespoons fresh lemon juice

¾ lb (375 g) lean bacon, cut into ¼-inch (6-mm) slices

2 chickens (3 lb/1.5 kg each), cut into serving pieces, breasts halved, wing tips removed

½ cup (2½ oz/75 g) all-purpose (plain) flour

kosher salt and freshly ground black pepper

¼ cup (2 fl oz/60 ml) cognac

4 cups (32 fl oz/1 l) dry red wine

8 cups (64 fl oz/2 l) chicken stock

¼ cup (2 oz/60 g) tomato paste

2 bay leaves

½ teaspoon dried thyme

16 cloves garlic, smashed and peeled

1 tablespoon chicken demi-glace

SERVES 6–8

American battery-raised chickens don't have the strong flavor of the old farmyard roosters typically used in rural French communities, so the intense demi-glace enriches this dish instead. Purchase it at well-stocked supermarkets. Use a good-quality wine for this dish.

1 In a large Dutch oven, melt ¼ cup (2 oz/60 g) butter over medium-high heat. Sauté onions until soft and browned, 5–7 minutes. Remove and set aside.

2 Toss mushrooms with lemon juice. In Dutch oven, melt remaining ¼ cup butter over medium heat. Sauté mushrooms over high heat until browned and cooked through, 7–10 minutes. Remove mushrooms and set aside. Add ⅔ cup (5 fl oz/160 ml) water, stirring to scrape up browned bits. Transfer deglazing liquid to a small bowl and set aside.

3 In Dutch oven, sauté bacon over medium heat until crisp, 7–10 minutes. Transfer to paper towels to drain. Leave 2 tablespoons fat in pot; add oil or pour off excess fat as necessary.

4 Rinse chicken pieces and pat dry. On a plate, combine flour and salt and pepper to taste. Coat chicken pieces well with flour mixture, shaking off excess. Heat reserved bacon fat in Dutch oven over medium-high heat. Working in batches, brown chicken pieces, about 10 minutes. Return chicken to pot.

5 In a small saucepan, warm cognac over low heat just until blue glints appear, 1–2 minutes. Ignite cognac, pour over chicken, and cook over low heat until flames die down, about 3 minutes. Remove chicken and add wine, stock, and mushroom deglazing liquid to pot. Stir in tomato paste, bay leaves, thyme, and 10 garlic cloves. Boil until reduced by half, about 30 minutes. Discard bay leaves. Return chicken to pot. Reduce heat and simmer, covered, until chicken is cooked through and tender, about 30 minutes.

6 Transfer chicken to a plate and keep warm. Skim off any grease from surface of sauce. Raise heat to medium and stir in demi-glace, 1 cup (8 fl oz/250 ml) boiling water, and remaining garlic cloves. Cook to reduce sauce to about 3 cups (24 fl oz/750 ml), about 15 minutes.

7 Strain sauce through a fine-mesh sieve. Wipe out pot. Return sauce to pot with garlic cloves. Taste and season with salt and pepper. Stir in chicken, mushrooms, onions, and bacon. Heat through.

Brined and Roasted Turkey

1½ cups (12 oz/375 g) sea salt or non-iodized table salt

1½ cups (12 oz/375 g) sugar

1 turkey (12–15 lb/6–7.5 kg)

2 tablespoons unsalted butter, softened, or 2 tablespoons extra-virgin olive oil

SERVES 8

Soaking turkey in a salt and sugar brine tenderizes and flavors it before roasting. Although time consuming, it is an easy process. Pan juices from a turkey brined in this manner will not be suitable for sauce or gravy, however. Serve the turkey with Bread Salad (page 94), the perfect match.

1 Bring 1 qt (1 l) water to a boil over high heat. Add salt and sugar and stir until dissolved. Remove from heat, cool, and stir together with 5 qt (5 l) cool water in a container large enough to hold turkey submerged.

2 Rinse turkey and pat dry. Place in brine to cover. Cure in refrigerator for 4–5 days. Drain, rinse, and dry well. Leave at room temperature for 1–2 hours before roasting.

3 Place a roasting pan in oven and pre-heat to 350°F (180°C) (this prevents the turkey from sticking to pan).

4 Pat turkey dry again. Rub turkey with butter or olive oil and place, breast side up, in preheated pan. Roast until an

instant-read thermometer registers 150°F (65°C) at the thickest point of a thigh, 1½–2 hours. If turkey isn't browning well, raise oven temperature to 400°F (200°C) when bird reaches an internal temperature of about 130°F (54°C).

5 Remove from oven and let rest for 20–30 minutes in a warm, draft-free spot. Discard the pan juices.

6 Remove legs. Using a boning knife, sep-arate thighs from drumsticks. If you like, slice leg meat off bones. Cut whole breasts from bone and then slice across grain.

Guinea Hen with Madeira and Dates

Seasoning the guinea hens 12-24 hours in advance helps develop flavor. Madeira is a fortified wine from the Portuguese island of the same name. Be sure to use dry, not sweet, Madeira.

2 guinea hens (3¼–3½ lbs/
1.6–1.75 kg each) cut into legs,
wings, and breast halves

4 teaspoons salt

1½ cups (12 fl oz/375 g)
chicken stock

2 tablespoons olive oil

6 bay leaves

1 cinnamon stick, broken into
a few pieces

4 whole cloves or allspice berries

1 cup (8 fl oz/250 ml)
dry Madeira

2 wide strips orange zest,
about 1½ inches (4 cm) long

16 small dates, pitted and halved

SERVES 8

1 Rinse guinea hen pieces and pat dry. Season with salt. Tuck each wing tip under top joint to form a flat wing. Cover hen pieces with plastic wrap and refrigerate until ready to cook.

2 Bring stock to a boil in a small saucepan over high heat. Reduce heat and simmer until liquid is reduced to about ⅔ cup (5 fl oz/160 ml), about 10 minutes. Set aside.

3 Place a rack in lower third of oven and preheat to 500°F (260°C).

4 Pat hen pieces dry again. Heat olive oil in a large ovenproof skillet over medium-high heat. Working in batches, brown skin side of hen pieces. Remove breast pieces and set aside. Turn over legs and wings, pour off excess fat, and tuck bay leaves, cinnamon pieces, and cloves beneath.

Transfer skillet to oven and roast for 15 minutes. Return breast pieces, skin side up, to pan, and roast until just cooked through, 8–10 minutes longer.

5 Transfer hen pieces to a platter and keep warm. Pour off excess fat from skillet and place over medium heat on stove top. Add Madeira and orange zest and, using a wooden spoon, scrape sides of pan and rub pan with orange zest. Bring to a boil. When wine has boiled hard for about 5 seconds, add reduced stock and dates. Return to a boil and cook, stirring often, until sauce has a little body and concentrated flavor, 7–8 minutes. Add a few drops of water if sauce becomes too concentrated.

6 Distribute hen pieces among warmed plates and spoon sauce and dates over.

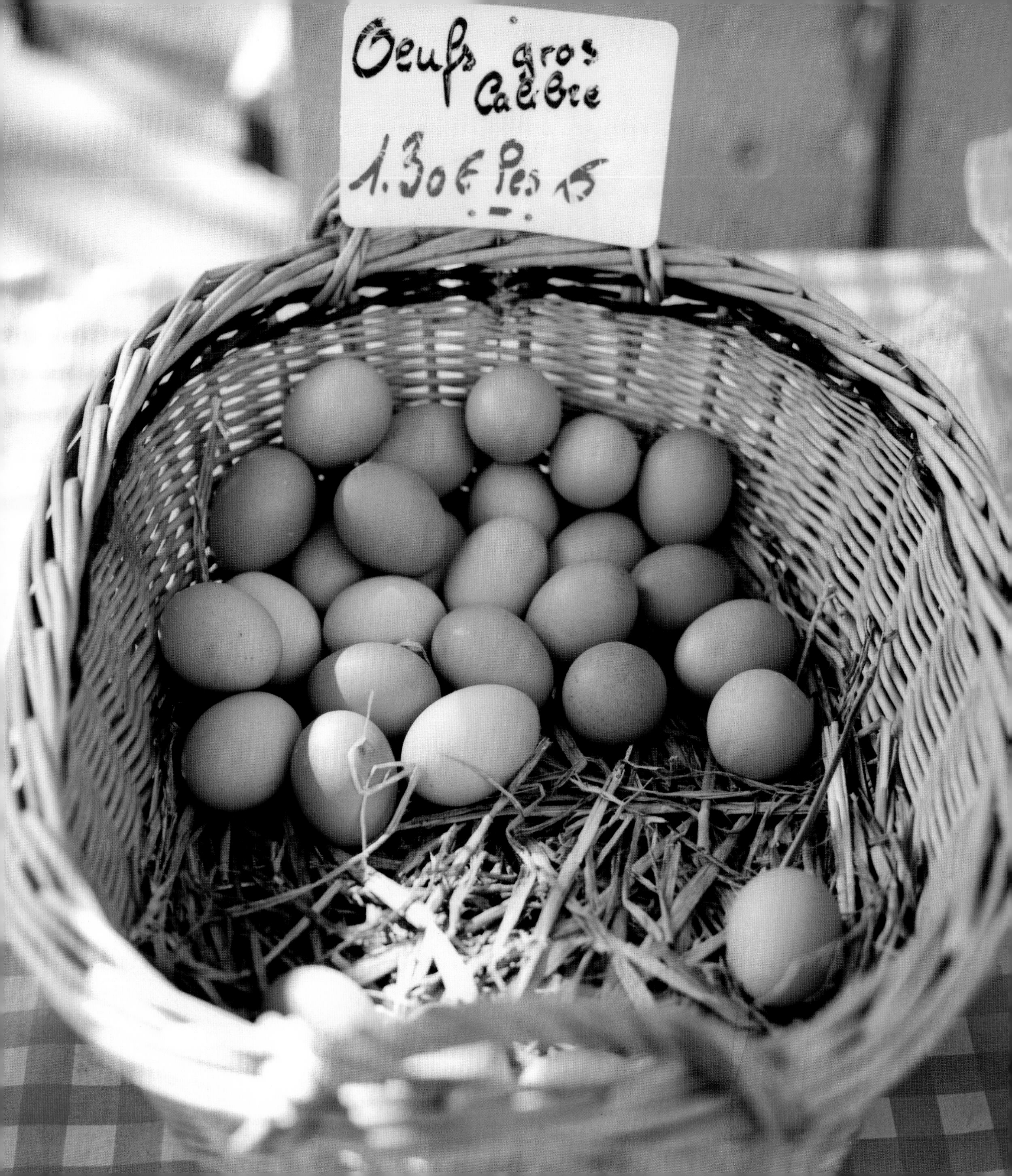
Oeufs gros Calibre
1.30€ les 15

Roasted Squab with Porcini Pearà Sauce

Squab can taste livery if cooked beyond medium-rare, so be sure to stop cooking when the meat is still a little rosy. Pearà sauce comes from the Veneto region of Italy and should be rich and peppery. For best effect, use coarse, fluffy bread crumbs from day-old bread.

8 squab (about ¾ lb/375 g each) wing tips removed

4 teaspoons salt

SAUCE

2 tablespoons unsalted butter

4 tablespoons (2 oz/60 g) rendered chicken or duck fat

1 large fresh porcino mushroom, cleaned and chopped, or 4 slices dried porcini, rinsed in warm water and chopped

1½ cups (3 oz/90 g) coarse fresh bread crumbs made from day-old chewy, white, peasant-style bread

freshly ground black pepper

1¼ cups (10 fl oz/310 ml) chicken stock, plus ¼ cup (2 fl oz/60 ml) if needed

¼ cup (1 oz/30 g) grated Parmigiano-Reggiano cheese (optional)

SERVES 8

1 Rinse and pat dry squab inside and out. Sprinkle each bird all over with ½ teaspoon salt. Cover loosely with plastic wrap and refrigerate. For best flavor, season 12–24 hours in advance.

2 Preheat oven to 500°F (260°C)

3 Pat squab dry again and place in a shallow baking pan, leaving room between so they brown evenly. Use a second pan if necessary.

4 Roast until the breast meat feels quite firm, about 12 minutes for medium-rare. Remove from oven and preheat broiler (grill). Slip pan(s) under broiler and broil (grill) until skins are browned, 2–3 minutes.

5 Let squab rest in roasting pans for about 5 minutes. Transfer to a platter and cover loosely with aluminum foil to keep warm. Reserve any pan drippings for pearà sauce.

6 FOR SAUCE: Place butter, rendered fat, and mushroom in a saucepan. Cook over medium-low heat, stirring constantly, until butter is melted. Raise heat slightly, add bread crumbs and a generous amount of pepper, and stir to incorporate. Stirring gently, add 1¼ cups stock and any degreased pan drippings from squab. Reduce heat to very low and cook about 3 minutes. Gradually add up to ¼ cup more stock if sauce is stiff. Don't overstir or overcook. Sauce should be texture of soft oatmeal. Remove from heat and stir in Parmigiano, if using. Taste and adjust seasoning.

7 Transfer squab to warmed individual plates, spoon pearà sauce over, and serve immediately. If necessary, hold sauce covered in a double boiler, over just simmering water, until needed. If sauce separates, stir gently and add a few drops of stock or water.

Basic Roast Goose

This simple method lets goose taste like goose, but produces a more tender, moister result than most recipes. Success depends on careful preseasoning with salt 3–5 days in advance; do not skip this step.

1 goose (10–14 lb/5–7 kg)

salt

STOCK

1 carrot, cut into chunks

½ onion, cut into wedges

1 bay leaf

3 black peppercorns

salt

SERVES 6–8

1 Rinse goose and pat dry. Trim off first 2 wing joints and neck and reserve for stock. Remove any pockets of fat.

2 Weigh goose and season with ¾ teaspoon salt per pound. Season thickest sections of leg or breast more heavily than ankles and thin sections of breast. Place on a platter or shallow roasting pan, cover loosely with plastic wrap, and refrigerate 3–5 days to allow salt to penetrate flesh evenly and thoroughly. Remove goose from refrigerator 1–2 hours before roasting.

3 Place a roasting pan in oven and preheat oven to 475°F (245°C) (this prevents the goose from sticking to pan).

4 Pat goose dry again and place, breast side up, in preheated pan. Roast for 30 minutes, then carefully spoon out accumulated fat from pan. (Reserve fat for other uses, if desired.)

5 Continue roasting until an instant-read thermometer registers 175°F (80°C) in breast and about 155°F (68°C) in thickest section of a thigh, about 1 hour. While goose is roasting, make stock.

6 FOR STOCK: In a saucepan, combine reserved goose parts, carrot, onion, bay leaf, and peppercorns. Add water to cover by ½ inch (12 mm). Bring to a simmer, skimming off any foam that rises to surface. Add a few pinches of salt. Cook at a gentle simmer until flavorful, about 45 minutes. (Watch that stock does not boil dry; add more hot water if needed.) Strain and set aside.

7 Remove goose from oven, transfer to a platter, and let rest for 20–30 minutes in a warm, draft-free spot.

8 Let fat settle in roasting pan, then pour off clear fat and discard, leaving darker juices in roasting pan. Add goose stock and simmer, stirring to scrape up browned bits from bottom of pan, until flavorful. Taste and adjust seasoning.

9 Remove legs. Using a boning knife, separate thighs from drumsticks. If you like, slice leg meat off bones. Cut whole breasts from bone and then slice across grain. Drizzle with deglazed pan drippings.

beef, pork & lamb

When it comes to the meat of the matter, the possibilities are truly endless. In this chapter, choose from quick stove-top dishes like Stir-Fry of Pork, Pistachios, and Peppers or those that require a little more time and attention, such as Ham and Stilton Risotto. The Lamb Shank and Red Lentil Soup with Quince and the Boeuf en Daube, like other robust soups and stews, require longer cooking but can be made ahead; their subtly nuanced flavors only improve with time. Such nourishing fare is guaranteed to warm the heart and feed the soul on a cold day.

Braised Pork Loin
with Orange

Cognac and orange add heady depth to this tender braise. Flambéing the cognac burns off most of the alcohol, leaving behind the flavor. Hold the lit match just above the liquor to light it. The flames should burn out in about 30 seconds. Serve with Mashed Rutabagas and Apples (page 107).

4 tablespoons (2 oz/60 g) unsalted butter

3 lb (1.5 kg) boneless pork loin, trimmed and tied

4 carrots, peeled and thinly sliced

1 teaspoon chopped fresh thyme

1 bay leaf

¼ cup (2 fl oz/60 ml) Cognac or brandy

1 cup (8 fl oz/250 ml) dry white wine, warmed

salt and freshly ground black pepper

3 oranges

SERVES 6

1 In a small saucepan, melt butter over low heat. Remove from heat and let stand for 1 minute to settle. Skim foam from top and discard. Pour clarified butter into a cup, leaving behind milky solids.

2 In a heavy Dutch oven just large enough to hold roast, heat clarified butter over medium-high heat. Brown pork loin well on all sides, 6–8 minutes. Transfer to a plate.

3 Add carrots and cook, stirring occasionally, until lightly browned, 2–3 minutes. Remove any excess butter. Add thyme and bay leaf and return pork to pot.

4 Pour Cognac into a ladle, heat over a burner, and ignite carefully, using a long match. Pour over pork. When flames die down, add wine and season with salt and pepper to taste. Reduce heat to medium-low, cover, and simmer until meat is very

tender and registers 155°–160°F (68°–71°C) on an instant-read thermometer, 1–1½ hours. Remove pork from pot and set aside on a plate. Cover loosely with aluminum foil to keep warm.

5 Discard bay leaf. Bring sauce to a boil over high heat and cook until reduced to about 1 cup (8 fl oz/250 ml).

6 Meanwhile, julienne zest from 1 orange. Simmer zest in a small saucepan of boiling water for 2 minutes. Drain. Squeeze juice from zested orange and add to sauce along with zest. Simmer over medium-low heat to blend flavors, 3–4 minutes.

7 Separate remaining oranges into segments. Remove strings from pork and place on a warmed serving platter. Drizzle sauce over and arrange orange segments on top.

Pork Loin Stuffed with Pistachios and Goat Cheese

A colorful, nut-studded filling adds both flavor and texture to lean pork. Serve this impressive entrée warm at your next dinner party or at room temperature as part of a casual buffet or elegant picnic.

2 tablespoons olive oil

1 onion, chopped

2 sweet Italian sausages (3–4 oz/90–125 g each), removed from casings

½ cup (2 oz/60 g) shelled whole pistachio nuts, coarsely chopped

1 tablespoon chopped fresh marjoram

2 cloves garlic, minced

½ cup (1 oz/30 g) fresh bread crumbs

3½ lb (1.75 kg) boneless pork loin

salt and freshly ground black pepper

2 red bell peppers (capsicums), roasted (page 125) and cut into thick strips

½ cup (2½ oz/75 g) crumbled goat cheese, well chilled

SERVES 6–8

1 Heat 1 tablespoon olive oil in a sauté pan until hot. Add onion and cook, stirring occasionally, until softened, about 5 minutes. Add sausage meat and cook, stirring to break into small pieces, until no longer pink, 7–10 minutes. Add nuts, marjoram, and garlic. Cook, stirring, until garlic is just fragrant, about 1 minute. Remove from heat and stir in bread crumbs. Set aside to cool.

2 Preheat oven to 425°F (220°C). On a sturdy work surface, place pork loin on its side and cut in half lengthwise, stopping about ¾ inch (2 cm) from opposite side. (Do not cut all the way through meat.) Open up pork as you would a book, cut side up, making one flat piece of meat. Flatten to an even thickness with a meat pounder. Season with salt and pepper. Arrange an even layer of roasted bell pepper strips, skinned side down, over surface.

3 Add goat cheese to sausage mixture and toss gently to mix. Spread an even layer over bell peppers, pressing down gently. Roll up pork, jelly-roll fashion, making a compact cylinder. Using kitchen string, tie securely at 1-inch (2.5-cm) intervals to close. Coat with remaining 1 tablespoon olive oil and season with salt and pepper. Place pork on a rack inside a shallow roasting pan and roast until nicely browned on outside and barely pink inside, about 1¼ hours. (Meat should register 140°F/60°C on an instant-read thermometer.) Transfer to a cutting board, cover loosely with aluminum foil, and let rest for 10–15 minutes.

4 Snip and discard strings before carefully cutting pork into slices ¾–1 inch (2–2.5 cm) thick. Arrange slices on a serving platter and serve warm or at room temperature.

Ham and Stilton Risotto

Arborio rice is an Italian short-grain rice used in risottos because it plumps nicely without breaking up or becoming mushy. Use it for this international twist on ham and cheese.

4½ cups (36 fl oz/1.1 l) chicken stock

1½ cups (6 oz/185 g) crumbled Stilton cheese

4 tablespoons (2 oz/60 g) unsalted butter

1 small onion, finely chopped

1½ cups (10½ oz/330 g) Arborio rice

2 oz (60 g) ham, shredded

freshly ground white pepper

SERVES 4

1 Place ½ cup (4 fl oz/125 ml) chicken stock and Stilton in a small saucepan and heat over low heat, stirring until Stilton melts into a sauce, about 5 minutes.

2 In a saucepan, bring remaining 4 cups (32 fl oz/1 l) stock to a gentle simmer over medium heat.

3 In a heavy-bottomed risotto pan or sauté pan, melt 2 tablespoons butter over medium heat. Add onion and cook, stirring often, until translucent and soft, about 5 minutes.

4 Add rice to pan and cook, stirring constantly, for 5 minutes.

5 Start to add hot stock a ladleful at a time, stirring well between each addition and adding next ladleful only when rice has absorbed the liquid. Continue adding stock and stirring continuously, until rice is al dente, about 20 minutes.

6 Stir in remaining 2 tablespoons butter, Stilton sauce, and ham. Sprinkle with white pepper and serve immediately.

Lamb Shank and Red Lentil Soup with Quince

2 tablespoons olive oil

2 lamb shanks, rinsed and halved through the bone crosswise

2 large onions, chopped

1 tablespoon ground turmeric

½ teaspoon ground cumin

2½ teaspoons salt

freshly ground black pepper

2 large or 3 smaller quinces, quartered, peeled, cored, and cut into large chunks

1 cup (7 oz/220 g) red lentils, picked over and rinsed

juice of 2 or 3 limes

1 tablespoon finely chopped fresh flat-leaf (Italian) parsley

¼ cup (⅓ oz/10 g) chopped fresh cilantro (fresh coriander)

yogurt, for serving (optional)

SERVES 4

This is an ideal main course to make in a slow cooker while you're away all day, for it's virtually impossible to overcook. Although it takes a few hours on the stove top, the soup doesn't require any attention during that time. Either remove the lamb from the bones after cooking and stir the meat into the finished soup, or serve a lamb shank half in each bowl. The quince will not turn pink, as it does in sweet preparations. Serve over rice, if desired.

1 Heat olive oil in a Dutch oven over high heat. Add lamb shanks and brown, turning often, until nicely colored, 8–10 minutes. Transfer lamb to a platter.

2 Reduce heat to medium-high and add onions, turmeric, cumin, salt, and pepper to taste. Cook, stirring occasionally, until onions are soft, about 5 minutes.

3 Return shanks to pot and add quinces, 2½ qt (2.5 l) water, and lentils. Bring to a boil, skimming any foam that rises to surface. Reduce heat and simmer, stirring occasionally, until lamb is tender, about 2 hours.

4 Remove shanks, cut meat from bone, shred meat, and return it to pot, if desired. (Alternatively, serve lamb on the bone, placing a piece in each bowl.) Stir up lentils to break them into a purée. Add lime juice to taste, to sharpen flavors. Stir in parsley and cilantro. Taste and adjust seasoning. Serve hot in shallow individual bowls, topped with a dollop of yogurt, if desired.

Agneau d'Haricot

2 cups (14 oz/440 g) dried navy or other small white beans, picked over and rinsed

1 bay leaf

3 fresh flat-leaf (Italian) parsley sprigs

1 large fresh thyme sprig

3 fresh sage leaves

3 tablespoons confectioners' (icing) sugar

2 teaspoons kosher salt

freshly ground black pepper

2 lb (1 kg) boneless leg of lamb, cut into 1½-inch (4-cm) pieces

2 tablespoons unsalted butter

2 onions, cut into 1-inch (2.5-cm) chunks

2 cloves garlic, smashed and peeled

2 large potatoes, peeled and cut into ½-inch (12-mm) chunks

½ cup (4 fl oz/125 ml) tomato purée

SERVES 6

Sugar is used in this dish not for its sweetness but to make a deep-tasting caramel flavor. Finely powdered confectioners' sugar does this most efficiently. If a thicker stew is preferred, finish off by stirring in a slurry of cornstarch (cornflour) and water and heat until thickened.

1 In a saucepan, bring 6 cups (48 fl oz/1.5 l) water to a boil. Add beans. Turn off heat. Let stand 30 minutes, then drain. Return beans to pan and add water to cover by 4 inches (10 cm). Bring to a boil. Reduce heat and simmer for 25 minutes. Drain. Rinse with cold water. Set aside.

2 Place a rack in lower third of oven and preheat to 350°F (180°C).

3 Using kitchen string or cheesecloth (muslin), tie together bay leaf, parsley, thyme, and sage. Set aside.

4 In a bowl, combine confectioners' sugar, salt, and pepper to taste. Add lamb and toss to coat.

5 In a Dutch oven, melt butter over medium heat. Working in batches, add lamb and onions and cook over high heat until well browned, 10–15 minutes. Be careful not to burn the sugar.

6 Stir in reserved beans, herb bundle, garlic, potatoes, tomato purée, and enough water to just cover. Cover and bake until lamb and beans are tender, 1¼–1½ hours. Remove herb bundle and discard. Taste and adjust seasoning with salt and pepper, if needed.

Boeuf en Daube

2 oranges

¼ cup (2 fl oz/60 ml) olive oil

3 lb (1.5 kg) beef chuck, trimmed
and cut into ½-inch (12-mm) slices
about 4 inches (10 cm) in diameter

2 yellow onions, halved and
thinly sliced

large pinch *each* of dried savory,
dried sage, and dried marjoram

¼ cup (2 fl oz/60 ml) pastis

⅔ cup (5 fl oz/160 ml) dry red wine

1 cup (8 fl oz/125 ml) beef stock

4½ teaspoons tomato paste

6 thick slices lean bacon

12 cloves garlic

4 fresh thyme sprigs

2 bay leaves

¾ cup (4 oz/125 g) green olives

6 oil-packed anchovy fillets,
drained and finely chopped

2 tablespoons drained capers,
rinsed

SERVES 6

Tradition dictates marinating the meat with wine and aromatics overnight before slow cooking for 4–6 hours in an earthenware *daubière* braising pot. This recipe uses a much faster cooking time with equal success. The olives in this dish are not pitted; smooth, green, salty picholines are ideal. Cognac can be substituted for the pastis.

1 Place a rack in lower third of oven and preheat to 325°F (165°C).

2 Remove 10 wide strips of zest from oranges, then juice oranges into a small bowl. Set juice and zest aside.

3 In a large skillet, heat olive oil over high heat until smoking. Add as many pieces of beef as will fit in a single layer. Cook over high heat, turning once, until browned, about 10 minutes. Transfer to a plate. Repeat with remaining beef.

4 Reduce heat to medium. Add onions to pan and cook until browned, about 7 minutes. Transfer to a bowl and stir in savory, sage, and marjoram. Set aside.

5 Pour off any remaining fat in skillet. Add pastis. Warm over low heat and ignite carefully, using a long match. Allow flames to die down. Add reserved orange juice, wine, stock, and any meat juices on plate, stirring to scrape up browned bits from bottom of pan. Stir in tomato paste. Remove from heat and set aside.

6 Layer bacon in bottom of a large Dutch oven, preferably stoneware or earthenware. Smash and peel garlic cloves. Finely chop 6 and leave 6 whole.

7 Starting with beef, alternately layer beef, whole garlic cloves, and onion mixture. Top with thyme sprigs, bay leaves, and orange zest.

8 Pour in deglazing liquid. Cover and bake until meat is tender, about 2½ hours.

9 Discard thyme sprigs and bay leaves. Spoon remaining cooking liquid into a saucepan. Skim off any excess fat. Add olives, chopped garlic, anchovies, and capers to saucepan. Bring to a boil, then reduce heat to low and simmer for about 5 minutes. Add olive mixture to stew. Serve directly from Dutch oven, or transfer meat to a serving dish and pour sauce over it.

Blanquette de Veau

¼ cup (1½ oz/45 g) all-purpose (plain) flour

kosher salt and white pepper

3 lb (1.5 kg) lean shoulder of veal

5 tablespoons (2½ oz/75 g) butter

½ cup (4 fl oz/125 ml) vegetable oil

1 *each* large carrot, onion, and leek

1 small turnip

2 celery stalks, coarsely chopped

4 cloves garlic, smashed and peeled

¼ cup (⅓ oz/10 g) fresh flat-leaf (Italian) parsley, chopped

1 bay leaf

1½ teaspoons chopped fresh tarragon

½ teaspoon fresh thyme leaves

½ lemon

2 cups (16 fl oz/500 ml) chicken stock

10 oz (315 g) button mushrooms

18 *each* baby carrots and pearl onions

2 egg yolks

½ cup (4 fl oz/125 ml) heavy (double) cream

SERVES 6

Blanquette, from Provençal *blanqueto* and French *blanc*, "white," is a stew of light meat or seafood in a white sauce. Be careful not to brown the veal, to ensure tender results and the traditional color of the dish. Serve with rice.

1 In a large bowl, stir together flour and salt and white pepper to taste. Cut veal into 1½-inch (4-cm) pieces. Add to flour mixture and toss to coat lightly. In a large Dutch oven, melt 4 tablespoons butter in oil over medium heat. Add veal and cook quickly in batches, turning often, until surface is white all over, about 10 minutes. Do not brown.

2 Transfer veal to a platter and set aside. Coarsely chop large carrot, onion, white part only of leek, and turnip and add to pot. Add celery, garlic, and parsley and cook until vegetables are softened, 5–7 minutes. Return veal to pot and add bay leaf, tarragon, and thyme. Using smallest holes on a box grater-shedder, finely grate zest from lemon half into pot; reserve lemon. Add stock to cover and simmer until meat is tender, 1–1¼ hours.

3 Meanwhile, wipe mushrooms clean and cut off stems flush with caps; discard stems. Place caps in a bowl and squeeze in 1 tablespoon lemon juice. Toss to coat. In a skillet, melt remaining 1 tablespoon butter over low heat and sauté mushrooms until cooked through, 5–7 minutes. Do not brown. Set aside.

4 Trim baby carrots. In a saucepan of lightly salted boiling water, blanch baby carrots and pearl onions until barely tender, about 8 minutes. Drain and rinse with cold water. Peel onions.

5 Using a slotted spoon, transfer veal to a dish with a lid and add baby carrots, pearl onions, and mushrooms. Cover and keep warm.

6 Strain cooking liquid and return to pot, discarding chopped vegetables and herbs. Skim off any excess fat. Bring to a boil over high heat and cook to reduce by one-third, about 10 minutes.

7 In a bowl, whisk together egg yolks, cream, and remaining lemon juice. Whisk in a ladleful of hot cooking liquid and then whisk cream mixture into cooking liquid over low heat. Do not boil; stir until thickened, about 5 minutes. Add veal and vegetables and cook until just heated through. Taste and adjust seasoning. Serve immediately.

Prosciutto and Gruyère Quiche

Prosciutto is a popular salted and air-cured Italian ham. Supremely rich, it is often used in paper-thin slices. Purchase it in a single chunk for this recipe, to cut into dice. Serve with baby salad greens.

all-purpose (plain) flour, for dusting

Pâte Brisée (page 124)

5 oz (155 g) prosciutto, diced

5 oz (155 g) Gruyère cheese, diced

1 cup (8 fl oz/250 ml) milk

1 cup (8 oz/250 g) crème fraîche

2 eggs, lightly beaten

salt and freshly ground black pepper

SERVES 6-8

1 On a lightly floured surface, roll out pâte brisée about ¼ inch (6 mm) thick and line a 12-inch (30-cm) metal tart pan with a removable bottom. Trim edge. Using a fork, prick base. Cover with plastic wrap and refrigerate for at least 1 hour or overnight.

2 Preheat oven to 375°F (190°C).

3 Place chilled tart shell on a baking sheet lined with parchment (baking) paper or aluminum foil. Line shell with parchment paper or aluminum foil and fill with pie weights or dried beans. Bake until sides are set, about 10 minutes. Remove weights and parchment or foil. Continue baking until bottom is set, 5–10 minutes longer. Remove from oven and let cool.

4 Raise oven temperature to 425°F (220°C). Arrange prosciutto and Gruyère in the baked tart shell.

5 In a bowl, stir together milk, crème fraîche, eggs, and salt and pepper to taste until combined. Pour into tart shell.

6 Bake until filling is just set and golden brown on the surface, 40–45 minutes. Let cool on a wire rack for 10 minutes before unmolding and serving.

Stir-Fry of Pork, Pistachios, and Peppers

Asian flavors and the crunch of bean sprouts, bell peppers, and pistachios enliven this simple stir-fry. Serve over rice, if desired.

2 tablespoons soy sauce

1 tablespoon firmly packed brown sugar

¼ teaspoon red pepper flakes

2 tablespoons vegetable oil

2 teaspoons peeled and finely diced fresh ginger

1 lb (500 g) pork tenderloin, cut into thin strips

1 red bell pepper (capsicum), seeded and cut into strips

3 green (spring) onions, cut into 2-inch (5-cm) lengths

1 cup (2 oz/60 g) bean sprouts

¼ cup (1 oz/30 g) pistachio nuts, coarsely chopped

SERVES 4

1 In a small bowl, stir together soy sauce, brown sugar, and red pepper flakes. Set aside.

2 Heat a wok or large skillet over medium-high heat. When hot, add 1 tablespoon oil. Add ginger and toss and stir until fragrant, about 30 seconds. Add pork and toss and stir until cooked through, 3–5 minutes. Transfer pork to a plate and set aside.

3 Add remaining 1 tablespoon oil to wok. When hot, add bell pepper and toss and stir until softened, about 5 minutes. Add green onions and bean sprouts and sauté for 30 seconds.

4 Return pork to pan. Add pistachios and soy sauce mixture and cook until sauce is reduced and glossy, about 1 minute. Serve immediately.

Pizza with Arugula and Prosciutto

PIZZA DOUGH

1 envelope (¼ oz/7 g) active dry
yeast (about 2¼ teaspoons)

¼ teaspoon honey

1 cup (8 fl oz/250 ml) plus
2 tablespoons lukewarm water
(about 105°F/40°C)

2 tablespoons dry white wine

3¾ cups (19 oz/590 g)
all-purpose (plain) flour,
plus more for kneading

5 teaspoons extra-virgin olive oil,
plus more for coating

¾ teaspoon fine sea salt

4 tablespoons (1½ oz/45 g)
cornmeal

6 oz (185 g) arugula (rocket),
tough stems removed

1 tablespoon fresh lemon juice

3 teaspoons extra-virgin olive oil

salt and freshly ground pepper

6 oz (185 g) thinly sliced prosciutto

SERVES 6

Taking the time to make a sponge in the morning so the dough can rise slowly throughout the day yields a dense, somewhat chewy crust with a distinctive, tangy flavor.

1 FOR DOUGH: To prepare sponge, in a large bowl, combine yeast, honey, and ¼ cup (2 fl oz/60 ml) of lukewarm water and stir until yeast is dissolved. Let stand until slightly foamy on top, 10–15 minutes. Add remaining water, wine, and ¼ cup (1½ oz/45 g) flour and whisk until smooth. Cover loosely and set aside in a warm place until foamy, 2–3 hours.

2 Add 2½ cups (12½ oz/390 g) flour to sponge, beating with a wooden spoon until smooth and well blended, about 5 minutes. Cover and set aside in a warm place until puffed but not necessarily doubled in volume, 2–3 hours.

3 Beat in 2 teaspoons olive oil and salt. Turn dough out onto a well-floured work surface and gradually knead in remaining 1 cup (5 oz/155 g) flour, or more if needed, turning and folding until dough is smooth and elastic, about 10 minutes. Roll dough into a cylinder and divide in half. Form each half into a disk. Place disks on

a well-oiled baking sheet, turning once to coat both sides. Cover and set aside in a warm place until puffed, about 1½ hours.

4 About 30 minutes before baking, position 2 oven racks in lower third of oven and preheat to 425°F (220°C). Sprinkle each of 2 large baking sheets with 2 tablespoons cornmeal. Roll or stretch each disk into a round 10–12 inches (25–30 cm) in diameter and place on prepared baking sheets. Brush each round with 1½ teaspoons olive oil. Bake until firm and barely golden at edges, 12–15 minutes.

5 Meanwhile, in a bowl, toss arugula with lemon juice and olive oil. Season with salt and pepper to taste.

6 Transfer pizzas to a cutting board. Top each with prosciutto and then arugula salad, dividing meat and greens evenly. Cut into pie-shaped wedges, transfer to warmed individual plates, and serve.

side dishes

The best side dishes are versatile, able to complement either a simple main course or a showstopper. In our choice selection of recipes, exotic vegetables are introduced, as in the Cardoon Gratin; fruits make an appearance, as in Savory Clafoutis with Prunes in Marsala; and more familiar produce takes on a sophisticated slant, as in Pearl Onions Glazed with Honey and Vinegar or Mashed Rutabagas and Apples. Familiar or new to you, the side dishes in this chapter provide strong and tasty support to all kinds of main dishes, or they can even star at the center of a meal.

Pearl Onions Glazed with Honey and Vinegar

A mix of tiny onions makes this a colorful side dish for grilled or roasted meats and poultry. Honey and currants in this preparation coax the sweetness of the onions forward to create a perfect savory/sweet balance.

1¼ lb (625 g) red pearl onions

10 oz (315 g) white pearl onions

2 tablespoons unsalted butter

1 tablespoon olive oil

2 fresh thyme sprigs

1 teaspoon finely chopped fresh rosemary

1 bay leaf

salt and freshly ground black pepper

3 tablespoons dried currants

1½ tablespoons buckwheat honey or other dark honey

3 tablespoons sherry vinegar

SERVES 4–6

1 In a saucepan of boiling water, working in batches, blanch onions for 1 minute. Drain and rinse with cold water. Using a small sharp knife, remove skin and tough outer layer of each onion. Make a small X in base of each onion.

2 In a wide nonstick skillet, melt butter in olive oil over medium-high heat. Add thyme, rosemary, and bay leaf, then onions. Cook, shaking pan occasionally, until onions are partially browned, 6–8 minutes. Season with salt and plenty of pepper, then add currants and enough water to cover onions a little more than halfway.

3 Cook, covered, until onions are tender, 7–10 minutes; add a little bit more water if needed.

4 Uncover and add honey and vinegar. Raise heat to high and cook, stirring constantly, until liquid is syrupy and onions are evenly glazed, about 5 minutes. Discard bay leaf and thyme. Season to taste with salt and pepper.

Bread Salad

This side dish is an excellent alternative to stuffing for serving with the Brined and Roasted Turkey (page 56). For the best texture, use chewy, peasant-style bread. Serve with handfuls of frisée, arugula (rocket), or other seasonal leaves tossed into the salad.

1 lb (500 g) day-old, chewy, peasant-style bread (not sourdough), crust removed

¾–1 cup (6–8 fl oz/180–250 ml)) mild-tasting olive oil

3 tablespoons champagne vinegar or white wine vinegar

salt and freshly ground black pepper

2 tablespoons dried cranberries

2 teaspoons red wine vinegar, plus more to taste

¼ cup (1 oz/30 g) pine nuts

3 cloves garlic, slivered

8 green (spring) onions, including pale green tops, thinly sliced

¼ cup (2 fl oz/60 ml) chicken stock

2 oz (60 g) frisée, torn into small pieces

SERVES 8

1 Preheat broiler (grill).

2 Cut bread into a couple of large pieces. Brush with olive oil and broil (grill) very briefly, to crisp and lightly color surface. Turn and crisp other side. Tear bread into irregular 2- to 3-inch (5- to 7.5-cm) chunks, bite-sized bits, and big crumbs. You should have about 8 cups.

3 Reduce oven temperature to 475°F (245°C).

4 Combine ½ cup (4 fl oz/125 ml) olive oil with champagne vinegar and salt and pepper to taste. Toss bread with vinaigrette in a wide bowl. Bread will be unevenly dressed. Taste one of the more saturated pieces. If bland, add a little salt and pepper and toss again.

5 Rinse dried cranberries under warm running water. Place in a small bowl and moisten with red wine vinegar and 3 tablespoons water. Set aside.

6 Place pine nuts in a small baking dish and bake for 2 minutes to warm through. Add to bread mixture.

7 Place 1 tablespoon olive oil in a small skillet, add garlic and green onions, and cook over medium-low heat, stirring constantly, until softened. Fold into bread mixture along with drained cranberries. Drizzle with chicken stock and fold again. Season with salt, pepper, and a few drops of red wine vinegar to taste.

8 Pile bread salad in a 2-qt (2-l) baking dish and tent with aluminum foil. Roast for 10 minutes. Turn oven off and leave to warm through, about 5 minutes. Just before serving, toss in greens, taste, and adjust seasoning. Serve in a warmed bowl.

Savory Clafoutis with Prunes in Marsala

Prunes prepared a few days ahead are even tastier. This dish is delicious served alongside simply roasted pork or poultry.

1½ cups (12 fl oz/375 ml)
Marsala wine

1 wide strip orange zest

¾ lb (375 g) pitted prunes,
about 2¼ cups

1¾ cups (14 fl oz/430 ml)
whole milk

1¾ cups (14 fl oz/430 ml)
heavy (double) cream

1 large fresh rosemary sprig

3 tablespoons cake flour
(not self-rising)

1½–2 tablespoons sugar

4 large eggs

1 egg yolk

salt

SERVES 8

1 In a small saucepan, warm Marsala with orange zest over medium heat. In a bowl, combine prunes and warm wine with zest and set aside to cool. (Prunes can be prepared and refrigerated up to 3 days ahead of using.)

2 In a saucepan, warm milk, cream, and rosemary over low heat. Remove from heat and let stand until milk is scented, about 10 minutes. Strain and let cool.

3 Preheat oven to 375°F (190°C).

4 Combine flour and sugar in a bowl. In another bowl, lightly beat eggs and egg yolk. Make a well in center of flour mixture and pour in eggs. Stir eggs, gradually incorporating surrounding dry ingredients.

5 Stir in milk mixture. Add a few pinches of salt to taste. If there are any lumps of flour, pass batter through a strainer.

6 Pour batter into a shallow 2-qt (2-l) baking dish or divide among 8 individual 1-cup (8–fl oz/250-ml) ramekins. Drain prunes, reserving Marsala mixture. Distribute prunes evenly throughout baking dish or divide among ramekins. Bake until lightly browned and puffy at edges and just set in center, 30–35 minutes for baking dish or about 25 minutes for ramekins.

7 Serve warm, drizzled with reserved Marsala mixture.

Classic Spätzle

Spätzle are tiny, wiggly, chewy dumplings. The name translated from Swabian dialect means "little sparrows." There are several types of spätzle makers available, or you can push the batter through a colander with ¼-inch (6-mm) holes.

salt

5 tablespoons (2½ oz/75 g) unsalted butter or 5 tablespoons (2½ fl oz/75 ml) olive oil

2⅔ cups (11 oz/345 g) cake flour (not self-rising)

4 large eggs

freshly ground black pepper (optional)

SERVES 6–8

1 Fill a wide sauté pan with water and bring to a boil over high heat. Add salt and 2 tablespoons butter. Adjust heat to maintain a brisk simmer.

2 Sift flour into a bowl with a pinch salt. Lightly beat eggs and pour over flour. Stir with a fork until eggs are just absorbed. Much of flour will still be dry and loose. Stir in ½ cup (4 fl oz/125 ml) lukewarm water to form a heavy, lumpy batter. Trickle in 2 more tablespoons water just until batter is soft and no longer holds a peak as you mix it. Batter should hang off fork for a second before dripping.

3 Spoon ½ cup (4 oz/125 g) batter into a spätzle maker or colander and set over the boiling buttered water. Working in batches, press batter (or, if using a colander, smear batter against the sides with a spatula), forcing it through holes. A batch should just crowd surface of water when they float up, about 30 seconds. Once they float, cook for 1 minute more. Lift spätzle out with a slotted spoon and shake gently to drain. Cool on a lightly oiled rimmed baking sheet. Repeat with remaining batter.

4 To serve, melt remaining 3 tablespoons butter in a large sauté pan. Add spätzle and cook, stirring occasionally, until heated through, 5–7 minutes. (Alternatively, heat pan juices from a roast in a large sauté pan. Add spätzle and cook, stirring occasionally, until heated through.) Taste and add salt and pepper if desired. Transfer to a warmed bowl and serve at once.

Beet Greens with Mustard, Horseradish, and Cream

The triple bite of bitter greens, sharp mustard, and fresh horseradish gives this richly colored side dish presence. A generous splash of cream unites and softens the flavors.

6 tablespoons (3 oz/90 g) unsalted butter

1 onion, diced

salt

1½ lb (750 g) trimmed beet greens or red chard, tough ribs removed and leaves torn

½ cup (4 fl oz/125 ml) heavy (double) cream or ½ cup (4 oz/125 g) crème fraîche or sour cream

2 teaspoons Dijon mustard

2 teaspoons freshly grated horseradish

freshly cracked black pepper

SERVES 8

1 Melt butter in a large sauté pan over medium heat. Add onion and a few pinches of salt and cook until onion is slightly softened, about 5 minutes.

2 Reduce heat to low and add beet greens. Stir to coat with butter, cover, and cook until limp, about 5 minutes.

3 Uncover pan and continue to cook greens, stirring occasionally, until dull green, soft and satiny, and cooked down to about 4 cups (28 oz/875 g), about 15–20 minutes. Stir in cream, mustard, and horseradish and cook for 5 minutes longer to allow flavors to blend. Add freshly cracked pepper and salt to taste.

Cardoon Gratin

Cardoons look a bit like overgrown heads of celery but are actually an unrefined, stalky relative of the artichoke. Look for firm, pastel green cardoons—whole heads or loose stalks—with fresh-looking leaves. Cardoons turn brown where trimmed, but that doesn't affect flavor.

1¼ lb (625 g) loose cardoon stalks, or 1 head (2 lb/1 kg), trimmed and separated into stalks, leaves and damaged parts removed

salt

½ cup (1 oz/30 g) fresh bread crumbs made from day-old, chewy, white peasant-style bread

6 teaspoons extra-virgin olive oil

2 tablespoons dry white wine or dry white vermouth

1 clove garlic, halved

1 cup (8 fl oz/250 ml) heavy (double) cream

3 salt-packed anchovy fillets, rinsed and pounded

½ cup (2 oz/60 g) grated Parmigiano-Reggiano cheese

freshly cracked black pepper

SERVES 4

1 Fill a stockpot with 4 qt (4 l) lightly salted cold water.

2 Taste a sliver of cardoon; occasionally it will be sweet—more often it will be somewhat bland or bitter. If bland or bitter, add cardoons to pot, bring to a simmer over high heat, then drain. Rinse and taste; if still bitter, repeat process, rinsing pot between blanchings, until no longer bitter, usually 2 or 3 times. Reduce heat slightly, add a few teaspoons salt to final blanching water, and let cardoons continue cooking until stalks are tender-crisp, 10–25 minutes. Do not drain. If cardoons are sweet initially, simmer just once until tender-crisp.

3 Remove from heat and let cardoons rest in cooking water for about 5 minutes. Drain and spread on paper towels. Trim any discolored parts. Strip prominent thick strings from stalks. Cut cardoons into ½-inch (12-mm) diagonal slices.

4 Preheat oven to 425°F (220°C).

5 Combine bread crumbs with 2 teaspoons olive oil and wine. Spread on a baking sheet and toast until barely golden and slightly crisp, about 5 minutes.

6 Rub inside of a shallow gratin dish with garlic and add cardoons.

7 In a small saucepan, stir together cream and anchovies and gently warm over medium heat. Stir in 2 tablespoons Parmigiano and pour over cardoons. Sprinkle with remaining cheese, drizzle with remaining 4 teaspoons olive oil, and sprinkle with toasted bread crumbs.

8 Bake until top is browned and juices are bubbly, about 20 minutes. Garnish with freshly cracked black pepper.

Mashed Rutabagas and Apples

Comfort foods combine in this hearty and flavorful fruit-and-vegetable purée scented with wine. Serve with pork chops or roast chicken or turkey.

3 lb (1.5 kg) rutabagas, peeled and cut into small chunks

salt and freshly ground white pepper

2 Granny Smith apples, peeled, quartered, cored, and cut into small chunks

3 tablespoons butter

1 tablespoon firmly packed brown sugar

2 tablespoons Madeira or sherry

freshly ground nutmeg

SERVES 6

1 Place rutabaga chunks in a saucepan with water to cover and add 1 tablespoon salt. Bring to a boil over medium-high heat. Reduce heat to low and cook, covered, until tender, 15–20 minutes. Drain and set aside.

2 Place apple chunks in saucepan with ⅓ cup (3 fl oz/80 ml) water. Bring to a simmer and cook, covered, until soft and transparent, about 8 minutes. Drain.

3 In a food processor, purée apples with rutabagas, working in batches, until smooth. Return purée to saucepan over medium heat. Add butter and brown sugar. Stir until well combined and hot. Season with salt and white pepper to taste. Stir in Madeira. Transfer to a serving dish and sprinkle with nutmeg.

Snow Peas and Pearl Onions

12 oz (375 g) pearl onions

1 lb (500 g) snow peas (mangetouts), trimmed

3 tablespoons unsalted butter

salt and freshly ground black pepper

SERVES 6

To trim snow peas, snap off the stems and pull the string from the shells. Be careful not to overcook, so the peas retain their bright green color and pleasant crispness.

1 Bring a saucepan of water to a boil. Add pearl onions and blanch for 3 minutes. Drain, rinse with cold water, and drain again. Using a small sharp knife, trim root end of an onion and squeeze from stem end. Onion will slip out. Repeat to peel remaining onions.

2 Bring a saucepan of water to a boil. Add peeled onions and cook over high heat for about 2 minutes. Add snow peas and cook until bright green, 2–3 minutes. Drain and return to saucepan. Add butter and salt and pepper to taste and toss to coat. Serve immediately.

Layers of Beans and Grains

7–8 oz (220–250 g) slab bacon

2 *each* onions and carrots

5 *each* whole cloves, fresh thyme sprigs, and bay leaves

¾ cup (5 oz/155 g) dried chickpeas (garbanzo beans), soaked overnight in cold water and drained

9½ cups (76 fl oz/2.4 l) chicken stock, plus more if needed

salt and freshly ground pepper

½ teaspoon ras el hanout

1 cup (7 oz/220 g) dried navy beans or other small white beans, soaked overnight in cold water and drained

2 shallots, finely chopped

¾ cup (6 oz/185 g) whole kamut berries, soaked overnight in cold water and drained

1 cup (7 oz/220 g) quinoa, rinsed several times in a fine-mesh sieve

freshly grated nutmeg

⅔ cup (4½ oz/140 g) small green French lentils du Puy

½ teaspoon sherry vinegar, plus more for serving

extra-virgin olive oil for serving

SERVES 8

Each type of bean and grain is cooked separately for optimum texture. Ras el hanout is a traditional Moroccan spice blend available in Middle Eastern stores.

1 Cut bacon into ¼-inch (6-mm) strips. Cut the carrots and onions into 1-inch (2.5-cm) chunks. Divide bacon strips, onion and carrot chunks, cloves, thyme sprigs, and bay leaves into 5 portions.

2 In a saucepan, combine chickpeas, 1 portion of bacon mixture, and 2 cups (16 fl oz/500 ml) stock and bring to a boil. Reduce heat to low and simmer for 1 hour. Season with salt to taste and ras el hanout. Continue cooking until tender, 30–60 minutes longer, adding more stock or water as needed. Drain; discard bacon, vegetables, herbs, and spices.

3 In a saucepan, combine navy beans, 1 portion of bacon mixture, and 2 cups stock and bring to a boil. Reduce heat to low and simmer for 45 minutes. Season with salt to taste. Continue cooking until tender, about 15 minutes longer, adding more stock or water as needed. Drain; discard bacon, vegetables, herbs, and spices. Stir in shallots and set aside.

4 In a saucepan, combine kamut, 1 portion of bacon mixture, and 2 cups stock and bring to a boil. Reduce heat to low and simmer for 25 minutes. Season with

salt to taste. Continue cooking until tender, about 10 minutes longer, adding more stock or water as needed. Drain; discard bacon, vegetables, herbs, and spices.

5 In a saucepan, combine 1 portion of bacon mixture and 1½ cups (12 fl oz/ 375 ml) stock and bring to a boil. Stir in quinoa. Cover, reduce heat to low, and simmer for 15 minutes. Remove from heat and let stand, covered, for 5 minutes. Discard bacon, vegetables, herbs, and spices. Season with salt and nutmeg to taste.

6 In a saucepan, combine lentils, remaining bacon mixture, and remaining 2 cups stock and bring to a boil. Reduce heat to low and simmer for 15 minutes. Season with salt to taste. Continue cooking until tender, 5–15 minutes longer, adding more stock or water as needed. Drain; discard bacon, vegetables, herbs, and spices. Season with ½ teaspoon sherry vinegar.

7 In a large glass bowl, spread lentils, kamut, navy beans, quinoa, and chickpeas in an even layer. Pass olive oil, vinegar, salt, and pepper at the table.

White and Green Asparagus with Romesco Sauce

Delicious with asparagus as well as most other vegetables, Romesco sauce is also a traditional Spanish accompaniment to fish and shellfish. White asparagus is harvested when the tips just break the ground. This lack of exposure to sunlight is responsible for their mild flavor and creamy color. Look for fresh white asparagus in specialty produce markets.

SAUCE

¾ cup (3½ oz/105 g) slivered almonds

2 ripe tomatoes, peeled (page 125), seeded, and coarsely chopped

1 red bell pepper (capsicum), roasted (page 125) and coarsely chopped

1½ tablespoons red wine vinegar

3 cloves garlic, chopped

salt

cayenne pepper

¾ cup (6 fl oz/180 ml) extra-virgin olive oil

2½–3 lb (1.25–1.5 kg) fresh asparagus, preferable a combination of green and white varieties, tough ends removed

SERVES 4–6

1 FOR SAUCE: Preheat oven to 350°F (180°C). Spread almonds in a single layer on a baking sheet or in a shallow pan. Bake, stirring once or twice, until lightly browned and fragrant, 5–10 minutes. Let cool.

2 In a blender or food processor, combine toasted almonds, tomatoes, roasted bell pepper, vinegar, garlic, ½ teaspoon salt, and ¼ teaspoon cayenne. Process until a coarse paste forms. With machine on, slowly add olive oil in a thin, steady stream. Process until well blended. Taste, adding more salt or cayenne as needed. Transfer sauce to a small bowl and refrigerate, covered, for at least 2 hours or as long as 2 days to blend flavors. Bring to room temperature before serving.

3 Bring a large shallow pot of lightly salted water to a boil over high heat. If asparagus spears are thick, use a vegetable peeler to trim base of each spear, starting about halfway down.

4 If using white asparagus, cook separately to avoid discoloration from green asparagus. Working in batches if necessary, add asparagus to boiling water and cook until spears are tender-crisp when pierced with tip of a knife, 3–5 minutes, depending on thickness.

5 To serve warm, drain well and serve at once. To serve cold or at room temperature, immediately plunge cooked asparagus into a large bowl of ice water to stop cooking. Drain well. Arrange asparagus spears in a shallow dish or serving platter. Pass Romesco sauce at the table.

Deep-Roasted
Fall Vegetables

1 lb (500 g) small white onions,
about 1¼ inches (3 cm)
in diameter

3 tablespoons olive oil, for coating

½ lb (250 g) carrots, peeled
and cut crosswise into 1-inch
(2.5-cm) slices

½ lb (250 g) broccoli florets

1 lb (500 g) yellow summer squash,
quartered lengthwise and cut into
1-inch (2.5-cm) pieces

2 tablespoons finely chopped
fresh marjoram

kosher salt and freshly ground
black pepper

SERVES 4–6

The dish works well for almost any kind of dinner party, whether served hot as a side dish with simple roasted meats or as a light vegetarian main course, or cooled and lightly dressed with a little more olive oil and some balsamic vinegar.

1 To peel onions, trim off top and root ends and make a small X in each root end. Drop into a pot of boiling water. When it returns to a boil, drain onions, plunge into cold water, and drain again. Slip off skins.

2 Place a rack in lower third of oven and preheat oven to 500°F (260°C). Coat bottom of a heavy 18-by-13-inch (45-by-33-cm) roasting pan with olive oil. Add onions and shake pan to coat them with oil. Roast for 7 minutes.

3 Shake pan to turn onions over. Move them to center of pan. Surround onions with carrots, broccoli, and squash. Roast for 15 minutes.

4 Turn vegetables over. Roast until browned and tender, about 7 minutes longer.

5 Sprinkle evenly with marjoram and roast for 3 minutes longer.

6 Season to taste with salt and pepper. Serve hot.

Savory Roasted
Apple Charlottes

A classic French dessert, charlottes are made in individual molds typically lined with ladyfingers or sponge cake. Here, a bread lining tips the balance back to a side dish savory enough to serve alongside pork or poultry.

FILLING

3½–4 lb (1.75–2 kg) apples such as Braeburn, pippin, Golden Delicious, or Gala

pinch of salt

1–2 teaspoons sugar

2 tablespoons unsalted butter, cut into small pieces

splash of cider vinegar (optional)

½ lb (250 g) chunk day-old, chewy, peasant-style bread, crust removed

4–6 tablespoons (2–3 oz/60–90 g) unsalted butter, melted

SERVES 8

1 Preheat oven to 375°F (190°C). Have ready eight 1-cup (8–fl oz/250-ml) ramekins.

2 FOR FILLING: Peel, core, and quarter apples. Toss with salt and sugar to taste. Spread apples in a crowded single layer in a baking dish. Dot with butter and cover tightly with aluminum foil. Bake until apples start to soften, 15–30 minutes, depending on type of apples.

3 Raise oven temperature to 500°F (260°C). Uncover apples and bake until tips are golden and fruit is tender, about 10 minutes.

4 Scrape apples into a bowl and stir into a chunky mash. Season with additional salt and sugar to taste and cider vinegar, if you like. Let cool.

5 Reduce oven temperature to 350°F (180°C).

6 Cut bread into slices ⅛ inch (3 mm) thick. (Partially freezing the bread may make this easier.) Using a paper template, cut 16 rounds from the bread to line ramekin bottoms and tops. Cut rectangles to line sides.

7 Brush one side of bread rounds with melted butter and place in ramekins, buttered side down. Set aside remaining rounds. Brush rectangles with melted butter and line sides, buttered sides against ramekin. Fill each ramekin with roasted applesauce and top with remaining rounds, buttered side up. Press down lightly.

8 Bake until golden brown, about 30 minutes. To serve, slide a knife around edge and turn out onto warmed individual plates. Charlottes should be golden all over with tasty caramelized spots where applesauce leaked through bread. Serve warm.

Butternut Squash with Wild Rice and Pecans

Wild rice is not a rice at all but actually the seed of an aquatic grass native to Minnesota, where it grows wild. Its extremely nutty flavor blends beautifully with roasted squash. Serve with poultry dishes such as Cornish Hens with Honey Glaze (page 51).

⅓ cup (2 oz /60 g) pecan halves

¾ cup (4½ oz/140 g) wild rice

salt and freshly ground
black pepper

1 tablespoon unsalted butter

2 butternut squash, about 1 lb
(500 g) each, halved and seeded

2 tablespoons olive oil

SERVES 4

1 Preheat oven to 350°F (180°C).

2 Toast pecans on a pie pan until fragrant, about 8 minutes. Let cool. Set aside 8 pecan halves. Coarsely chop remaining pecans.

3 In a bowl of cold water, rinse wild rice, skimming off particles on surface. Drain.

4 In a saucepan, bring 4 cups (32 fl oz/ 1 l) water to a boil. Add wild rice and ¼ teaspoon salt. Cook, covered, over medium heat until grains have split, about 45 minutes. Drain. Stir in butter and chopped pecans. Season with salt and pepper to taste.

5 Meanwhile, raise oven temperature to 400°F (200°C). Rub cut sides of squash with olive oil, season with salt and pepper, and place, cut sides down, on a baking sheet lined with parchment (baking) paper. Roast until tender and slightly caramelized, 30–35 minutes.

6 Fill squash cavities with wild rice and garnish with reserved pecan halves.

Roasted Cherry Tomatoes with Orange and Cardamom

Tiny cherry tomatoes, such as Sweet 100s, work best for this recipe. The addition of cardamom adds a lemony note that pairs well with the orange zest. Try serving the tomatoes with fluffy couscous and crisp-skinned roasted chicken.

4 cups (1½ lb/750 g) cherry tomatoes, stemmed

1½ tablespoons olive oil

¼ teaspoon kosher salt

5 strips orange zest, each ¼ inch (6 mm) by 3 inches (7.5 cm)

5 cloves garlic, each smashed and cut into 4 pieces lengthwise

2 teaspoons cardamom seeds

SERVES 4–6

1 Preheat oven to 500°F (260°C).

2 Put tomatoes in a roasting pan. Add olive oil and shake pan to coat tomatoes thoroughly. Sprinkle with salt.

3 Roast for 10 minutes. Shake pan to turn tomatoes. Tuck orange zest, garlic, and cardamom seeds underneath tomatoes. Roast until tomatoes start to collapse, about 15 minutes longer. Serve immediately.

Crunch Dough

2½ cups (12½ oz/390 g) all-purpose (plain) flour

½ teaspoon sugar

1½ teaspoons salt

¾ cup (6 oz/185 g) cold unsalted butter, cut into ½-inch (12-mm) cubes

MAKES ONE 12-BY-4-INCH (30-BY-10-CM) TART SHELL

This dough, which produces a short crust, is best made a day ahead. It can be used for savory and sweet preparations.

1 In bowl of a stand mixer fitted with paddle attachment, combine flour, sugar, and salt and beat on low speed. Add half of butter and combine until pea-sized bits form, about 30 seconds. Add remaining butter and combine as before, about 1 minute. Stir in ⅔ cup (5 fl oz/160 ml) cold water and mix until large lumps form. Turn out onto a lightly floured surface. Using your hands, bring mixture together to form a rough dough.

2 Gently knead with heel of your hand until dough is just barely homogenous, about 20 seconds. Flatten into a disk, wrap in plastic wrap, and refrigerate for at least 1 hour or preferably overnight.

Pâte Brisée

2½ cups (12½ oz/390 g) all-purpose (plain) flour

¾ teaspoon salt

10 tablespoons (5 oz/155 g) cold unsalted butter, cut into ½-inch (12-mm) cubes

1 egg, lightly beaten

½ teaspoon fresh lemon juice

MAKES ONE 10- TO 12-INCH (25- TO 30-CM) TART SHELL

This dough is the classic savory pastry of France, though recipes vary from cook to cook. In this version a squeeze of lemon juice is added to sharpen the buttery flavor.

1 In bowl of a stand mixer fitted with paddle attachment, combine flour and salt. Add butter and beat on low speed until mixture resembles fine bread crumbs, about 1 minute. Add egg, ¼ cup (2 fl oz/60 ml) cold water, and lemon juice and mix until large lumps form. Turn out onto a lightly floured surface. Using your hands, bring mixture together to form a rough dough.

2 Gently knead with heel of your hand until dough is just homogenous, about 30 seconds. Flatten into a disk, wrap in plastic wrap, and refrigerate for at least 1 hour or preferably overnight.

Roasting Bell Peppers

1 Preheat broiler (grill). Place bell peppers (capsicums) on a broiler pan and broil (grill), turning them often, until charred on all sides.

2 Slip peppers into a paper bag and let them steam for a few minutes, then peel off blackened skin. (Do not rinse the peppers, or you will wash away flavor; a few black specks are acceptable.)

3 Remove stems and seeds, and cut peppers into long, narrow strips.

Peeling and Seeding Tomatoes

1 Bring a saucepan of water to a boil. Using a sharp knife, score a shallow X in blossom end of each tomato. Immerse tomatoes in the boiling water and leave for 15–30 seconds, or until skins just begin to wrinkle.

2 Remove tomatoes with a slotted spoon, let cool slightly, then peel away skins.

3 Cut in half crosswise and squeeze gently to dislodge seeds.

index

acknowledgments

Weldon Owen would like to thank the former TASTE magazine editorial and design teams for their creative efforts. Special thanks to the many talented authors and photographers who contributed so greatly to this book. And, finally, thanks to Peggy Fallon, Tanya Henry, Joan Olson, Victoria Spencer, Richard Van Oosterhout, and Juli Vendzules for their valuable assistance.

credits

AUTHORS: **CHAMPAGNE VEUVE CLIQUOT:** Page 88; **ALAIN DUCASSE** and Spoon Food & Wine, Paris: Page 113; **PEGGY FALLON:** Pages 33, 70, 114; **ANDY HARRIS:** Pages 15, 16, 34, 38, 43, 44, 47, 52, 73, 87; **BARBARA KAFKA:** Pages 23, 55, 77, 80, 83, 117, 122; **DEBORAH MADISON:** Pages 19, 29, 51, 74, 93, 121; **PASCAL RIGO:** Pages 20, 37, 84, 124; **JUDY RODGERS:** Pages 56, 59, 62, 65, 94, 97, 98, 103, 104, 118; **CHUCK WILLIAMS:** Pages 69, 107, 108; **MICHAEL YEAMENS:** Page 26.

Savory Roasted Apple Charlottes, Guinea Hen with Madeira and Dates, Roasted Squab with Porcini Pearà Sauce, and Classic Spätzle, adapted from *The Zuni Cafe Cookbook* by Judy Rodgers.

PHOTOGRAPHERS: **ANTONIS ACHILLEOS:** Pages 50, 57, 58, 63, 64, 96, 119; **SANG AN:** Pages 100, 101 (top right); **QUENTIN BACON:** Pages 27, 78 (top left), 110 (bottom right); **BEN DEARNLEY:** Page 101 (bottom left); **MIKI DUISTERHOF:** Page 25; **MICHAEL FREEMAN:** Pages 24 (top left, top right, bottom right), 40; **DANA GALLAGHER:** Pages 12, 21, 36, 85; **SHERI GIBLIN:** Endpapers, Pages 92, 95, 99, 102, 105, 106, 109, 120; **RICHARD JUNG:** Page 9; **DAVID LOFTUS:** Cover, Pages 10, 32, 71, 86, 110 (top right, bottom left), 112, 116, 123; **CHARLES MARAIA:** Page 78 (top right); **WILLIAM MEPPEM:** Pages 8, 14, 17, 18, 24 (bottom left), 28, 35, 39, 42, 45, 46, 53, 60, 61 (top left, top right, bottom left, bottom right), 68, 72, 75, 76, 78 (bottom right), 79, 89, 101 (top left, bottom right), 109, 110 (top left); **MICHAEL PAUL:** Pages 1, 6, 54, 78 (bottom left), 81, 82; **LUCA TROVATO:** Pages 22, 111; **ROGER STOWELL:** Page 115.

WILLIAMS-SONOMA INC.
Founder & Vice Chairman: Chuck Williams

WILLIAMS-SONOMA TASTE
Editor-in-Chief: Andy Harris
Art Director: Emma Ross
Original Design: Martin Welch

WELDON OWEN INC.
Chief Executive Officer: John Owen
President and Chief Operating Officer: Terry Newell
Vice President International Sales: Stuart Laurence
Sales Manager: Emily Jahn
Creative Director: Gaye Allen
Publisher: Hannah Rahill
Associate Creative Director: Leslie Harrington
Associate Publisher: Val Cipollone
Art Director: Kari Ontko, India Ink
Assistant Editor: Mitch Goldman
Copy Editor: Carrie Bradley
Proofreader: Desne Ahlers
Indexer: Ken DellaPenta
Production: Chris Hemesath, Teri Bell

Recipes and photographs originally published in the USA, 2000-2002, in Williams-Sonoma TASTE Magazine © 2000–2002 Weldon Owen Magazines Inc. and Williams-Sonoma Inc.

MAIN COURSES & SIDE DISHES
Conceived and produced by Weldon Owen Inc.
814 Montgomery Street, San Francisco, CA 94133
In collaboration with Williams-Sonoma Inc.
3250 Van Ness Avenue, San Francisco, CA 94109

Printed in China by Midas Printing Limited

A WELDON OWEN PRODUCTION
Copyright © 2004 Weldon Owen Inc. and Williams-Sonoma Inc.
All rights reserved, including the right of reproduction in whole or in part, in any form.

First printed in 2004
10 9 8 7 6 5 4 3 2 1

Library of Congress Cataloging-in-Publication Data is available

ISBN 1-740895-25-8